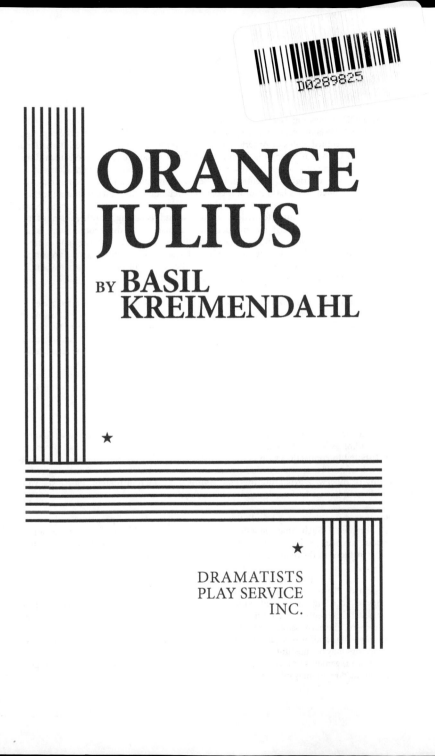

ORANGE JULIUS

BY **BASIL KREIMENDAHL**

DRAMATISTS
PLAY SERVICE
INC.

SPECIAL NOTE
Anyone receiving permission to produce ORANGE JULIUS is required to give credit to the Author as sole and exclusive Author of the Play on the title page of all programs distributed in connection with performances of the Play and in all instances in which the title of the Play appears, including printed or digital materials for advertising, publicizing or otherwise exploiting the Play and/or a production thereof. Please see your production license for font size and typeface requirements.

Be advised that there may be additional credits required in all programs and promotional material. Such language will be listed under the "Additional Billing" section of production licenses. It is the licensee's responsibility to ensure any and all required billing is included in the requisite places, per the terms of the license.

SPECIAL NOTE ON SONGS AND RECORDINGS
Dramatists Play Service, Inc. neither holds the rights to nor grants permission to use any songs or recordings mentioned in the Play. Permission for performances of copyrighted songs, arrangements or recordings mentioned in this Play is not included in our license agreement. The permission of the copyright owner(s) must be obtained for any such use. For any songs and/or recordings mentioned in the Play, other songs, arrangements, or recordings may be substituted provided permission from the copyright owner(s) of such songs, arrangements or recordings is obtained; or songs, arrangements or recordings in the public domain may be substituted.

The Off-Broadway premiere of ORANGE JULIUS was produced by Rattlestick Playwrights Theater (Daniella Topol, Artistic Director; Annie Middleton, Managing Director) and Page 73 Productions (Michael Walkup, Producing Artistic Director; Jennifer Lagundino, Managing Director), opening on January 22, 2017. It was directed by Dustin Wills, the set design was by Kate Noll, the costume design was by Montana Blanco, the lighting design was by Barbara Samuels, the sound design was by Palmer Hefferan, the projection design was by Joey Moro, the prop design was by Raphael Mishler, the production stage manager was Nicole Marconi, the assistant stage manager was Corinn Moreno, and the production manager was Rebecca Key. The cast was as follows:

NUT .... Jess Barbagallo
JULIUS .... Stephen Payne
FRANCE .... Mary Testa
CRIMP .... Irene Sofia Lucio
OL BOY .... Ruy Iskandar

ORANGE JULIUS received its world premiere on September 26, 2015, by Moxie Theatre Company (Delicia Sonnenberg, Executive Artistic Director), in San Diego, California. It was directed by Will Davis, the set design was by Victoria Petrovich, the lighting design was by Jason Bieber, the sound design was by Emily Jankowski, and the costume design was by Jennifer Brawn Gittings. The cast was as follows:

NUT .... Rae K. Hendersen
JULIUS .... Jeffrey Jones
FRANCE .... Dana Case
CRIMP .... Wendy Maples
OL BOY .... Steve Froehlich

ORANGE JULIUS was developed during a residency at Eugene O'Neill Theater Center's National Playwrights Conference (Preston Whiteway, Executive Director; Wendy C. Goldberg, Artistic Director) in 2012.

CHARACTERS

NUT, a young trans-masculine person.
Tough and masculine.

JULIUS, Nut's father, a man in his fifties – sixties.

FRANCE, Nut's mother, a woman in her fifties – sixties.

CRIMP, Nut's sister, a woman in her mid-thirties.
Feminine sexuality, but tough working-class.

OL BOY, a young man in his early twenties.
He's a hyper-masculine figure of Nut's creation.

TIME

Present.

"One night, like a piece of shrapnel that takes years to work its way out, I dreamed and saw a field that was crowded with dead bodies"

—Michael Herr,
Dispatches

ORANGE JULIUS

NUT. I was driving in the car with my dad. I'm seven, or six, nine maybe eight.

Julius sits down next to Nut.

My dad and I are driving past Johnson's Pond. I'm thinking about how I haven't learned to ice skate. How I've never actually been to Johnson's Pond. How it's like a building I don't ever have any business at. I say:

How come I've never been ice skating?

JULIUS. I swore I'd never take any of you kids, after what happened last time I took your brother and sister.

NUT. What happened?

JULIUS. Some kid fell down and another kid ran over his finger with their ice skate. Chopped it right off.

NUT. Oh.
That can really happen?

JULIUS. Yeah it can. It did.

NUT. Oh.

My dad smiles at me and he puts his hand on my knee. Kindly, he pats my knee and rubs it. I stiffen up. Why does this feel weird? Is this weird? This is the 1980s, and at school they make us watch Shari and Lamb Chop and at home we watch Afterschool Specials. But what exactly is inappropriate touch anyway? No one ever really said. Just that it could be anyone. It could be someone you trust. And it's probably going to be a man. I think he knew I got weirded out. Then I think he got weirded out. He put his hand on the steering wheel. Ten and two.
That was the last time he ever tried to be affectionate at all, and that was fine with me. You know, maybe... I don't know, maybe if he'd patted me on the back or shook my hand it wouldn't have felt so... like I was a little girl, it wouldn't have felt so off.

When I would eat plain potato chips after eating spaghetti, I would throw up.

France enters. She wipes it up.

My mother always had to clean it, because my father had a weak stomach.

He'd end up vomiting himself. You'd think a man who'd been through the Vietnam War could stomach some fucking puke, right?

But if I was bleeding my mother would faint and my father would laugh. Like when a stray fishing hook in the back of his car ripped through my finger. Stitches worthy. He laughed.

JULIUS. Here. Wrap this around it.

NUT. An oil-soaked car rag. Nice.

I thought that was pretty badass. I woulda kept that oil- and blood-soaked car rag on my finger for weeks. Woulda taken it off, reeeeal sloooooww and showed everyone my enormous gaping meat exposed wound. Instead.

FRANCE. Jesus Mary and Joseph, put a Band-Aid on that.

NUT. *The Karate Kid*'s a big hit and my sister's got a boy in our basement.

CRIMP. Get outta here! Little shit.

NUT. He's real cool. They move the rug and push all the furniture aside and he teaches her how to spin on the floor. He does martial arts and he breakdances.

I wanna learn karate.

JULIUS. You better go. This better not be like the clarinet.

NUT. I wanted to play the drums or the saxophone. But my dad had an old clarinet.

FRANCE. If you learn the clarinet then we will buy you the instrument you want. It's too expensive for something you won't stick with.

NUT. It's still the eighties, and my sensei hires the scariest woman in the world. A midget woman with teased out bleach-blonde hair and blue eye shadow up to her forehead. She leads class and says things like "drop and give me twenty." I decide to stop going.

JULIUS. I told you I'd punish you.

NUT. He belts me in the hallway, but my sister runs out of the bathroom.

CRIMP. How would you like it if I took that belt and hit you?

NUT. He apologized to me. He was ashamed. The man had a quick temper. Usually it was more like

Can you drive me to my friend's house?

JULIUS. Jesus fuckin Christ! It's my day off! No, I'm trying to relax.

NUT. I learned to just not say anything and go to my room. It wouldn't be more than five minutes later and he'd knock on my door and say

JULIUS. Put your shoes on. Let's go.

NUT. I always wondered if his temper came from whatever happened to him in Vietnam.

I'm twelve, fourteen maybe thirteen.

Julius sits next to Nut. He's wearing a Marines camo jacket.

I'm driving in the car with my dad. I just bought a new cassette tape.

Nut begins singing along with an early-'90s grunge song, such as "Wargasm" by L7.*

JULIUS. Does your mother know you listen to this?

NUT. What's that? On your jacket.

JULIUS. This?

NUT. Yeah.

JULIUS. Blood.

NUT. He smiles at me, because it's rust. But for a moment I wished he'd been telling the truth.

I wish those spots woulda been blood he'd carried around for over twenty years. I wished Vietnam was spilled all over his jacket. Then I could've asked

Whose was it? Then I could've asked

Did you do it? Then I could've asked. Then I could've asked. Then I could've asked.

---

* See special note on songs/recordings on page 55.

Lights up on Julius.

JULIUS. Why doesn't anyone ever hug me anymore?

I can't think straight anymore. I've been…I've been out of it.

NUT. Somewhere in Vietnam there's a woman. She was born on the exact same day as me, at the exact same moment. Her father, like mine, was exposed to Agent Orange. Only he never got to leave. Long dead by now. Cancer. And this woman was born with her eyes popped out of her head. Her face forever locked in a look of pure terror. No eyelids. Just popped out. Popped out all the time. No closing them, she'll never not see even when what she sees is too much.

Something that feels like orange powder, or maybe it is orange powder, falls from the sky. It covers the stage. There's an image or a sound from one of the Vietnam movies Nut watched with their dad.

Shift: Vietnam. Julius, Nut, and Ol Boy. It's almost as if Ol Boy has been summoned by the sound or image from the film. This feels almost like a Vietnam vaudeville act.

OL BOY. Fuck that. Crack that shit. You're fine motherfucker. Fuck I'm fine. Fuck you're fine. Check that shit. Check this shit out.

NUT. Fuck. You think they was scared?

Puts a cigarette in Julius's mouth.

Fuck yeah I was scared. I was fuckin scared.

(To Julius.) Were you scared?

OL BOY. *(To Julius, lighting his cigarette.)* You don't look scared. Fuck you don't look scared.

Cigarette falls out of his mouth.

NUT. I was fuckin scared.

Puts the cigarette back in Julius's mouth.

OL BOY. Fuck yeah they were scared.

Lights the cigarette again.

You could see that. You could see that plain.

Cigarette falls out of his mouth.

Fuckers quakin. You know?

Puts the cigarette back in Julius's mouth.

Fuckers shakin. Quakin and shakin.

(To Julius.) Not you, man. Not you. You didn't look scared.

Cigarette falls out of his mouth.

NUT. Fuck it man.

OL BOY. If fear hadn't frozen all the water I had left in me. Any was left. Pissed myself. I'd a fuckin pissed myself.

NUT. I ain't scared for nothin.

OL BOY. Buuuul-shieeet you wasn't scared.

NUT. No fuckin shit's gonna hit me in Vietnam.

OL BOY. Oh yeah?

NUT. Yeah.

OL BOY. And why the fuck is that you tell me why the fuck that is?

NUT. 'Cause it don't exist.

(To Julius.) You wasn't scared. Were you?

Silence.

OL BOY. This guy? This guy?

He smacks Julius, who comes to slightly.

You weren't scared

He smacks him again and Julius nods his head.

You weren't scared were you?

He smacks him again.

JULIUS. Nah

OL BOY. What?

JULIUS. Nah!

NUT. Nah!

OL BOY. Nah!

JULIUS. Nah nah nah nah! Nah!

He stands up and his legs are shaking so bad they buckle and he falls to his knees. Ol Boy starts laughing as he fades out. Bleed: Memory.

NUT. You can't stand up on your own anymore, for Christ's sake.

Don't you get that?

Nut props him up.

FRANCE. Can you watch your father? All you have to do is make sure he doesn't fall and hurt himself. You'll be fine. I've got to run some errands. I've just got to. I've got to. To get out. I have to. You'll be fine.

NUT. Please don't stand up.
There. Stay. Stay. Down boy. Stay.
It's just you and me. It's just me.

Silence.

There aren't any phone calls.

I was eight or nine when my parents separated. Not because of but maybe propelled by my father's altercation that led to the death of my grandmother's boyfriend, Billy. My dad had gone over to mow her lawn.

JULIUS. Billy was a drunk.

NUT. So you hit him.

JULIUS. Well, yeah. He was bad-mouthing your grandmother so I hit him. I punched him. But he was fine.

NUT. What'd he say about her?

JULIUS. Nothin worth repeating.

NUT. Punched him in the face.

JULIUS. He deserved it. And he was fine. When I left he was fine.

You know, Billy always acting like he was some kinda war hero, said he had a metal plate in his head from Vietnam. When they did that autopsy, they found out he didn't have one. And also that he'd sat behind a desk for the whole war.

FRANCE. He doesn't like to talk about it, but your father did get a few medals.

NUT. *(To audience.)* I always liked my grandmother's boyfriend Billy. I thought he was funny. He would make like his finger was missing and then pull my nose.

JULIUS. Your mother never wanted you around him.

12

NUT. 'Cause he was always drunk.

JULIUS. The guy would have seizures just walking down the street.

NUT. My dad got charged with manslaughter and lost his job of twenty years at the factory, because of the newspaper articles. VIETNAM WAR HERO MURDERED by some guy.

Around the same time. My parents meet in a park.

FRANCE. I think we should separate.

NUT. Then it's just my mother and me and we're watching a movie about men in prison. There's an incident in the shower.

FRANCE. Oh, Jesus! Don't! Oh god. Don't drop the soap.

NUT. What's that mean?

FRANCE. Oh, it's…it's so they don't…bend over.

NUT. Why?

FRANCE. Well, because they could get…raped.

NUT. I'm still nine or ten, I'm driving in the car with my mom and she tells me that my dog, who stayed with my father, got shot while out in the woods during hunting season, and that another dog laid its body on his doorstep.

I burst into tears, I thought for my dog, but really because I hoped my dad wouldn't drop his soap.

JULIUS. Billy went to bed that night. Had a seizure. Went into a coma and died. He was fine when I left.

NUT. After five years of court setbacks, the case was dismissed. He never spent any time in prison.

I'm twelve, thirteen maybe fourteen and my parents get back together.
In those five years I'd changed, I didn't look the same anymore, and before he came I guess, I'd been…the man in my mother's house. So it was like we were strangers to each other.
Not that he'd ever *not* really been a stranger. He'd always worked the graveyard shift so I don't remember seeing him much. But I do remember being in kindergarten or first or second grade. Standing outside the locked door, banging the door and ringing the door-

13

bell. He was supposed to wake up to let me in the house after school, but often...he'd forget.

I grew up not knowing why my mother married a man like him.

FRANCE. I married your father because I thought he could teach me how to have fun.

NUT. Oh yeah?

FRANCE. Mmhm.

But I don't think anyone can really teach you that.

NUT. She also told me that her and my dad used to drive to Plymouth Rock. They would sit on one of the benches that faced the water and watch the boats. They went because they liked to dream about how when they won the lottery, they'd buy a sailboat. For a moment they'd live a picture postcard life.

While they were separated I found a box with a stack of photographs. Saigon. The jungle.

I'm twelve years old. I have a small photograph book. Each page fits only one five-by-seven.

Its shiny plastic cover has flowers and an Asian lady on it, and it's stuffed with something that makes it puffy. There are photographs from a fifth-grade party in it. We played spin the bottle and it was very traumatic. I spent a long time getting ready. I spent a long time trying to look like a girl. I spent a long time looking awkward. I don't much care for them anyway, so I pull each one out and replace the pages with these black and whites. And when my dad comes to live with us again, I can't wait to show him.

JULIUS. That's where we used to shower. Yeah. You pulled this cord and the water fell out onto you.

That's our bunker.

I don't remember who that is.

NUT. It's a young black guy with an M16 standing guard on a rooftop. There is a long stretch of rooftops.

Who's this?

JULIUS. I don't remember.

NUT. It's my dad and another white guy with two Vietnamese women at a bar. I think he looks like a movie star. I don't believe a word he says. I tell him:

I've saved all these photos in this book for you, so they won't get lost.

JULIUS. Okay.

NUT. The next time I went to look at the photographs, the book was lost. I never got to look at the Vietnam photos again and I don't know where the traumatic-fifth-grade-party photos are.

When I was eight, nine, my sister gets a crimping iron and a set of assorted plates that iron your hair into various waves. And I got a training bra.

I don't think I really need this.

CRIMP. It's good to start early.

NUT. It's only because in gym class we all have to change in front of each other now.

CRIMP. You've got good boob genes.

NUT. What?

CRIMP. They'll get bigger, don't worry.
Fuckin Rita. Last year she went on and on about how she had the biggest boobs in school. I was like, really? Have you seen these? So we got out the ruler. It was kinda hard to figure out, but we measured them. Mine were bigger—You should let me crimp your hair!

NUT. No thanks.

CRIMP. Hey, Dad. Wouldn't Nut's hair look good crimped?

JULIUS. Sure it would.

CRIMP. She won't let me.

JULIUS. Why don't you let your sister crimp your hair.

NUT. No.

JULIUS. Why not?

NUT. I don't want it.

CRIMP. Your hair is getting so long.

NUT. It's annoying.

JULIUS. Your hair's pretty.

NUT. I wanna cut it all off.

JULIUS. You want people to think you're a boy?

NUT. I don't know. I don't know. I don't know.

I had a mini nervous breakdown once, okay twice. I'm fourteen.

FRANCE. This book here says that you should count how long you're breathing in and then count how long you're breathing out.

NUT. What?

FRANCE. Just breathe normal! Breathe how you breathe and count the in-breath and the out.

Nut does.

NUT. Yeah?

FRANCE. Well?

NUT. Seven in and four out.

FRANCE. So this says that means you're taking in too much oxygen.

NUT. I think I need past life regression. I've found someone who does it.

FRANCE. You should breathe in for a count of nine and out for a count of ten.

NUT. I have the number written down.

FRANCE. Try that.

NUT. This could be about something that happened in a past life. I read it in a different book.

FRANCE. We can't afford that. Just try this book. Breathe the right way.

Silence.

NUT. Can I sleep on your floor?

I had a memory once that wasn't mine, or maybe I made it all up because my father made me watch *Platoon*, *Full Metal Jacket* and *Apocalypse Now* every single year on Veterans Day when they all played on television. He always said *Platoon* was the most realistic.

The memory happened when I'd hurt my ankle. I don't know how or exactly how old I was, but I was taller than both of my parents.

FRANCE. Julius! Help her up the stairs. She's sprained her ankle.

NUT. I put my arm around my dad for support.
We take a step. Then without a word he puts my arm in a different position. It's almost like we're hugging. Immediately. I get this memory, a knowing that this is the proper procedure for carrying the wounded. It just feels like it.
    Shift: Vietnam.
Then I am in the jungle with him and he's carrying me out.

OL BOY. You got your deck this time?

NUT. I got my fucking deck. Lady cards. Look.

OL BOY. Shut the fuck up deal your deck let's play.

JULIUS. I wanna play.

OL BOY. You got your fucking deck?

JULIUS. Yeah.

OL BOY. We're playing Hill. Every motherfucker has to have his own deck. You got your fucking deck?

JULIUS. Yeah.

OL BOY. What color is it?

JULIUS. Red.

OL BOY. That's the color of my deck.

JULIUS. So?

OL BOY. So? So?

NUT. Everyone has to /

OL BOY. You gotta have your own color.

NUT. Or your own lady cards. See.

OL BOY. You gotta have like black or blue. 'Cause mine are red.

JULIUS. I got blue.

OL BOY. Okay, man. Outtasight. We're playin Hill motherfuckers. You played this before?

JULIUS. I don't remember.

OL BOY. It's a fast game. You're basically playing solitaire only all the aces get played on by everyone. The first person to get rid of all their cards, their hill...wins. So you gotta be like lightning quick and shit, you know? Like you runnin through the jungle.

NUT. "You better run through the jungle."

OL BOY. Nobody wants to hear you singin shit.

They play.

NUT. Julius likes it when I sing, dontcha?

JULIUS. It's alright. I like the lion song.

OL BOY. Lion song?

JULIUS. You know, lion sleeps tonight song.

OL BOY. That song is so not boss.

NUT. Yup. This card is my favorite card.

OL BOY. Huh.

NUT. What? You don't like this card?

OL BOY. She's alright.

JULIUS. She's fine.

NUT. See! She's fine. Fine.

JULIUS. That card's a keeper.

NUT. I know, right?

JULIUS. You find a keeper like that, well, then you gotta know how to keep it.

NUT. Yeah, like buy her shit.

Ol Boy laughs.

What?? You gotta buy her stuff, right? Like earrings or some shit.

JULIUS. That's not it /

NUT. Well then what?

JULIUS. I don't know. It's more like paying the right amount of attention. Not too much not too little.

NUT. Oh yeah like opening the door. Yeah.

OL BOY. Man, you couldn't keep / a

NUT. Shutup! You wouldn't know a keeper if she licked your face.

OL BOY. You're gonna suck it.

NUT. You wish.

OL BOY. You keep that up. You keep that up, I'll tell the sergeant about your numbers racket.

NUT. Yeah? What's he gonna do…send me to Vietnam?

JULIUS. You guys smell that smoke?

NUT. No.

OL BOY. I don't like the smell of this.

> *Bleed: Memory.*

Napalm? Napalm!

FRANCE. Are you sure you want to play?

JULIUS. Yeah.

CRIMP. He says he wants to play. Just let him.

> *The four play Hill. Julius is not really playing. He holds his cards, just staring at them.*

FRANCE. I was reading this magazine, ten cheap and easy wood projects.

NUT. Yeah?

CRIMP. That sounds nice.

FRANCE. I think there was a shelf you would like.

NUT. Hmmm.

JULIUS. You guys smell that?

CRIMP. No.   NUT. No.

FRANCE. There was also a bench I think I want to make. I could put it in the hallway.

JULIUS. You guys don't smell that smoke?

CRIMP. No, Dad.   NUT. No.

FRANCE. A ton of flower pots. I don't have any use for flower pots.

CRIMP. No.

FRANCE. The bench though, I could paint something on it, or decoupage.

JULIUS. You guys really don't smell that smoke?

FRANCE. I have this book with lots of illustrations all for decoupaging. I've been wanting to use them.

CRIMP. Oh, yeah?

JULIUS. That's smoke. I'm pretty sure that's smoke. You guys really don't smell it?

CRIMP. No!   NUT. No!

FRANCE. It looks really nice. I can show it to you later.

CRIMP. Okay.

JULIUS. I'm getting the fuck out of here!

FRANCE. What?

JULIUS. Yeah. I win!

> *He throws all of his cards all over the table and exits. France, Crimp, and Nut start laughing. They laugh so hard.*

FRANCE. It's really not funny.

CRIMP. Not at all.

NUT. I know.

CRIMP. "I win."

> *They laugh more.*

FRANCE. Your poor father.

> *They laugh so hard they cry.*

NUT. A year before my dad got sick it was my grandmother.

FRANCE. She keeps asking me to take her out with the garbage.

NUT. So she got the doctor to prescribe my grandmother antidepressants, then my mom hid them in her brownies.

FRANCE. I can't stand it anymore.

NUT. She died in our house. In her bed. It was my mother who took care of her too. I helped to change her Depends once, and I said I love you for the first and last time.

When she died my mother was holding her face and wiping her mouth and telling her it was okay while she choked on the foam coming up from her lungs.

I wrote a song about it. The song was called "Lubee in Search of Her

Feet." Because my grandmother had a giant round stomach and skinny legs. And I wondered if she wondered what her feet looked like as she laid in her bed.

Hospice came and brought her a wheelchair and a bed.

Hospice came and brought my dad a recliner and a bed.

FRANCE. Help me get your father into the bed.

NUT. This is silly. I can just pick him up.

FRANCE. No!

NUT. Just let me pick him up and put him in the bed. He's not that heavy.

FRANCE. You're his daughter.

NUT. But I've been working out.

FRANCE. No! You can't...*pick* up your father!

JULIUS. It's intestinal cancer. It was intestinal cancer. Now it's liver cancer. It's the ammonia from my liver in my brain. I can't think straight anymore. I've been...I've been out of it.

NUT. I'm twenty-one, twenty-two, I'm driving in the car with my dad, and I'm clean and sober. He asks

JULIUS. So how much does someone have to drink? I mean let's say someone has a beer every night after work. Does that mean he's an alcoholic?

NUT. I guess it depends.

JULIUS. On what?

NUT. If he HAS to have the one beer or not.

JULIUS. Even though he only has one?

NUT. I guess. I don't know.

I don't know who he's asking about, and I didn't ask. I didn't ask, not because I didn't want to know, but I don't know...maybe I didn't know how.

A woman told a story in a meeting about trying to make amends to people she'd done wrong. One of them was her father. She visited him in the hospital. She told him how sorry she was for all the trouble she'd caused and how she'd embarrassed him. The only thing was, was that her father had had tongue cancer and his tongue had been removed. So he couldn't ask her anything. He couldn't even say whether he forgave her or not.

I'm seven. I'm watching a TV show with my sister. It's an Afterschool Special. There's a teacher, dead, face down on his desk.

What happened to him?

CRIMP. He swallowed his tongue.

NUT. You can do that?

CRIMP. Yeah.

NUT. For several years after, I slept with a pencil in my mouth. So if I started to swallow my tongue I could just pull the pencil and pull my tongue out from the back of my throat.

    Shift: Vietnam.

OL BOY. *(To Nut.)* You don't know fear man. You don't know fear. You fuckin don't know fear till you know.

NUT. Amen!

OL BOY. When it's your motherfuckin life on the line. Then. Then you check it check yourself feel yourself all up and it's all still there. Then you know bliss man. You know bliss. You fuckin don't know till you know it.

JULIUS. I think that part's turned off.

NUT. Huh?

JULIUS. Yeah. It's turned off. The bliss part. I just got the fear part. Even when I check and I'm all still there. I'm just afraid.

    Silence.

OL BOY. Hey.
Y'all hear about that crazy motherfucker. Scooter or some shit.

NUT. Crazy fucker.

OL BOY. Fuckin crazy. Now that's the kind a crazy I say keep the fuck over there. Keep the fuck over there away from this motherfucker.

NUT. That's the kind a crazy sticks a grenade on the latrine door. You go take a fucking shit and Boom KAaaaBOOM! Right like that.

OL BOY. Right like that?

NUT. Yeah, right like that. KAaaBOOM!

OL BOY. KAaaBOOM?

NUT. Yeah.

OL BOY. Don't talk to me. Just don't even talk to me anymore.

(Interrupting Nut so they can't talk.) Jus…ah…ah…don't…talk to me.
> *Silence.*

You know why I'm not talkin to you.

NUT. What?

OL BOY. *(Shutting Nut up.)* Ah. Ah…
(To Julius.) So I'm walkin back to the bunker and I hear all those fools in C company hollerin out "Lifer! Nut's a lifer!" I said to myself what the fuck? That fucking fool.

I know what you did.

NUT. It's not that big a deal…

OL BOY. Don't even talk to me. Don't even fuckin talk to me. 'Cause you know what you are? You know what you are?

Dead man walkin. That's what you are. You like a ghost to me. I don't even see you.
(To Julius.) You on the other hand.

JULIUS. Yeah?

OL BOY. You getting outta here soon, and I know you ain't stupid enough to change that.

JULIUS. Nah.

OL BOY. Man knows what's good for him.

JULIUS. Yeah.
> *Silence.*

When I get home. Gonna eat a steak. Fuck my girl. Man…I got lots of things on my list.

OL BOY. Signed up for more time. Now who the fuck /
> *Nut pauses the imagining.*

NUT. Or maybe…

Rewind.

OL BOY. ...cuff ahth owe woN. mite roarmm rof puh ddnighS

JULIUS. .ttsil eyem nah sgith fa ssstall tog I naM. moe teg I nehw...
naM. llirg eyem cufF. kates a tee anoyG

Silence.

.heeaY

OL BOY. .mih rof doog s'taw sswohn naM

JULIUS. .hahN

Redo.

OL BOY. You gonna get outta here soon, and I know you ain't stupid
enough to change that.

JULIUS. Nah.

OL BOY. Man knows what's good for him.

JULIUS. Yeah.

Silence.

When I get home. Everything's gonna be so good.

OL BOY. Signed up for more time. Now who the fuck /

Nut pauses it again. That wasn't it.

NUT. Or maybe...

Rewind.

OL BOY. ...cuff ahth owe woN. mite roarmm rof puh ddnighS

JULIUS. .ttsil eyem nah sgith fa ssstall tog I naM.

Silence.

.heeaY

Redo.

OL BOY. Man knows what's good for him.

JULIUS. Yeah.

Silence.

When I get home. I'm gonna drive my car. That's what I want, just
drive my car. Drive down to the Cape. Roll the windows down.
Turn the radio up. Lean back. Turn the radio all the way up. Up up
up turn it up.

24

Bleed: A memory within an imagining.

Julius sings a popular oldie, like "Duke of Earl."* (Nut should finish speaking before Julius finishes singing.)

NUT. I'm driving in the car with my dad. I'm six, eight, or seven. I'm seven, eight, or six. We're driving in the car together we're speeding through a field the grass is really tall he's driving a Rabbit a little silver or gray Rabbit we're speeding through this field on a dirt road the grass is high wicked high the grass grows all the way up to the windows on the car we got the windows rolled down and and it's autumn it's autumn and the grass is wheat the grass is like hay or wheat we're speeding through this field and the wheat is reaching up over the car windows which are down and I got my arm out the window the grass is hitting my arm and my hand stinging the air smells good and it's not too cold and not too hot we've got the radio on and the windows down the radio's playing [the song sung above]
I'm driving in the car with my dad and it's...

great.

　　Shift: Vietnam.

JULIUS. Man...when I get home. Everything's gonna be so good. Man I got lots of things on my list.

OL BOY. Signed up for more time. Now who the fuck...
Three days to go home and you sign on for more?

NUT. Maybe some of us just got more a what it takes to be a soldier. It's no big deal. Just two months.

OL BOY. Two hours is too fuckin much. What's wrong with you

NUT. Maybe I just got more a that than you two.

OL BOY. Shit.

JULIUS. I shouldn't have been a soldier.

　　Silence.

I wet myself.

OL BOY. Shutup.

NUT. You're fine.

* See special note on songs/recordings on page 55.

JULIUS. *(To Nut.)* I'm not as much a man as you. I'm not. Men don't wet themselves.

OL BOY. *(Grabs Julius.)* I said, shutup! I'll fuckin /

NUT. Back off man.

OL BOY. I think you need a good ole /

NUT. I said back /

OL BOY. I'll fuckin knock some sense into /

JULIUS. Hey hey /

> *All three end up wrestling with each other. The lights change. Dark. Orange. Yellow. White. Bombs are exploding in silence. The three are silent and move slowly. The end result is all three changing from wrestling to holding on to one another. Bleed: Memory.*

NUT. At five *The Last Unicorn* was my all-time favorite movie. A unicorn, the only one left in the entire world. Searching for her kind. Who have all been destroyed by the fiery red-orange bull that chases them all down. Consumes them.

I saw it more times than I can count and the only image I remember is her, the unicorn, being chased down a dirt road in the jungle by the orange bull on fire.

This boy at school called me a dog.

CRIMP. That's why you should brush your hair.

NUT. She did. It was a scene straight out of *The Color Purple*

AGGHHHHHHHHH!
AGGHHHHHHHHH!
AGGGHHHHHH!   JULIUS. AGGGHHHHH!

> *Crimp has a small stuffed animal that plays a lullaby when you squeeze it. She holds it up to Julius's ear. He tries to brush it away.*

JULIUS. AGGGHHHHHHH!

CRIMP. This was my favorite song when I was a baby.

> *Julius turns away.*

26

You used to sing it to me.
When I was a baby it'd put me right to sleep.

She squeezes the doll again.

FRANCE. Your father never sang you to sleep.

CRIMP. Yes he did.

FRANCE. Your father never sang you to sleep.

CRIMP. He did.
It's one of my fondest memories of him.

FRANCE. The way you remember him…sometimes, I think you must've grown up in a different house.

CRIMP. He was the best.

She squeezes the stuffed animal.

To put me to sleep.

She squeezes it again.

You remember?

She puts it to his ear.

Do you remember?
You used to sing to me, to put me to sleep.

She squeezes it again.

JULIUS. *(Pushes the stuffed animal away.)* I just want to sit on the couch with my wife!

FRANCE. Okay. Alright. He's just…he's just tired.

JULIUS. I just want to sit on this couch with my wife.

FRANCE. I know.

JULIUS. I don't want to go anywhere.

NUT. But we go.

We go to the jetty in Cape Cod. I'm ten… Maybe and I haven't seen my dad in a year. The jetty stretches out into the Atlantic. A curved strip of boulders, rocks all piled onto one another. You can walk along the rocks but it's

FRANCE. It's treacherous. Oh god, please be careful.

NUT. There are all these tiny snails attached to the rocks. Hundreds of them all over.

JULIUS. They're periwinkles. You can eat them.

NUT. What? Eat them?

JULIUS. Yeah escargot. Snails. You've never heard of that? Yeah, you can eat them. It's a delicacy.

NUT. *(To the audience.)* I know about snails you can eat, and I don't think these are them.

(A dare, to Julius.) Can we eat them?

JULIUS. I just said you could.

NUT. Yeah but can we? Eat them…now?

JULIUS. Well…I guess we could.

NUT. Can we?

JULIUS. Yeah, sure. We can just boil them up. Put some crushed red pepper in it.

NUT. We do. Only they prove hard to eat. Toothpicks to pluck out their tiny snail bodies.

Chewy little gobs of nothingness.

We only went once or twice, but the jetty stuck to me.

I'm twenty. This old astrologer dyke takes me to a group meditation on past life regression given by the astrology association. We all sprawl out in someone's living room and this guy leads us through the meditation.

Think of someone who bothers you. See them. Go to them. Give them good feelings.

Now you are flying. Flying high above the scene and then to somewhere else.

Think of a place that makes you feel good and safe. Imagine all of its details.

I dream about the jetty. The boulders when it's warm. How I want to be alone sunning on one of the flat tops of a giant rock. The water pushing and slapping up against them. Pushing and slapping.

Somewhere along the way we end up somewhere else that is supposed to be this past-life image. All I can do is look down at my feet. No matter how hard I try I can't look around at anything else or even see any other part of me. The ground looks like a desert only the sand is different. More like dirt. A few small clumps of it scattered here and there. And my feet are not my feet. They're bigger, broader, boxier. My skin is darker more olive.

I'm in a—my hands and head are locked in the stocks. Like *The Scarlet Letter* and shit. Only the world around me is too dry for rotten tomatoes. And I'm definitely a man.

> *Shift: Vietnam.*

OL BOY. *(To Nut.)* Don't be a pussy...be a dick. That's all I'm sayin on the matter.

JULIUS. Don't be a dick. Jesus, don't listen to this guy.

NUT. What then?

JULIUS. Letters. Letters.

OL BOY. I hate to be the one ta break it to you, but letters don't replace bodies.

JULIUS. Letters, trust me.

NUT. Write letters. I do, I do that.

JULIUS. You gotta put your whole body in the letters. Like that.

NUT. Yeah?

JULIUS. Yeah. I don't know about fighting but I do know about this.

OL BOY. *(To Nut.)* She is fuckin some other guy. I am tellin you!

> *Orange powder falls on the three of them. Lights change to show us that they're now covered in oil.*

NUT. What the...what the fuck what's this shit what the fuck is this shit what the fuck is this shit what the fuck is this shit?

OL BOY. Just some shit, is all. Calm the fuck down.

> *Julius wipes his skin. Wipes his skin more. More frantically. Wiping and scrubbing.*

Motherfuckers don't tell a grunt shit. Could be droppin napalm, playin cowboys and Indians right up to the tip a your toes, grunt wouldn't know it till he's lookin up the barrel of an M16. Won't know shit till the mine explodes and you thrown back wondering why you got chunks of wet bits and shit all over your face.

29

NUT. Oh fuck. I think this shit's gonna explode or something. You know? Like this oil shit's gonna suddenly catch on fire. Fuck I bet that's what they're doin. Some new shit that just suddenly combusts.

OL BOY. Some chopper just dropped its load is all.

NUT. Its load of combustible oil bomb.

OL BOY. Prolly just its oil. Will you quit it! Fuckin quit rubbin that shit. God damn. You see me rubbin this shit off? I ain't rubbin it off. Look at me man, I'm all oiled up oiled up and fired up. This shit makes me feel like a warrior. Greased up and ready to fuck shit up, hear me?

NUT. I don't know.

OL BOY. That's your problem, right there.

You don't know how to see shit from the right angle. This is like… this is like them body builders. You know they get all greased up to look bigger and tougher. That's us right now. Bigger and tougher.

GREASE ME UP MOTHERFUCKERS.

Come on y'all.

GREASE. ME. UP MOTHERFUCKERS.

Come on.

NUT. GREASE ME UP MOTHERFUCKERS.

OL BOY. There you go. Come on now. Do it!

NUT.	OL BOY.
Do it. Do it. Do it. Do it.	Do it. Do it. Do it. Do it.

JULIUS. GREASE ME UP / MOTHERFUCKERS.

> *They hear something and before Julius can finish Ol Boy puts his hand over Julius's mouth and takes him down to the ground. Julius starts to sob.*

OL BOY. Shhh. Shh.

> *Long silence.*

NUT. Wadn't nothin.

OL BOY. Some four-legged thing. Maybe.
Gonna get dark soon.
You alright man you alright.

JULIUS. I'm fine.

OL BOY. I don't wanna be out here when night falls.

JULIUS. Won't be better up the way.
Let's just camp here.

OL BOY. See! All your foolin around. Now it's dark and we're in the middle of the fucking rat's nest with big ol cheese niblets around our necks.

JULIUS. I think when I get home I want a piece of pie.

OL BOY. Pie? Fuck that. Not me, no fucking American apple pie for me. I want a cheeseburger. Like a real one. Like a real McDonald's hamburger. Cheeseburger.

NUT. I'll just stick to this prepackaged grunt gruel.

OL BOY. What?

NUT. Yeah, man. I like it. What?

OL BOY. You just get worse by the day!

NUT. Nothin tastes quite like this.

OL BOY. No shit.

NUT. A taste you'll reenlist for!

OL BOY. Whatever.

NUT. So I was thinkin, we gotta get down. Show this guy a good time before he leaves. You know?

OL BOY. We're on a mission, okay? We're just escorting this mother-fucker to Da Nang. He's gonna get on his chopper and go where he belongs, outta here.

NUT. He's gotta have a little fun before he goes.

OL BOY. Fun? What fun?

JULIUS. This oil's soaked right through my pants to my legs.

    Bleed: Memory.

NUT. My dad's wearing shorts. That's never a pretty sight. Especially not now. All swollen and purple. His legs are splotched with hair. His mother is naturally hairless on her arms and legs. And she has indented nipples, which I found out when I was fourteen and visiting with her. I was watching *Basic Instinct*. I thought I was alone

31

and that she was sleeping in her bedroom, then suddenly I hear her voice, and she's sitting on the sofa right fucking next to me saying, "I wish my nipples looked like that."

Why is the hair on your legs like that?

JULIUS. Agent Orange defoliated me.

NUT. It's 2004.

FRANCE. Listen, your father and I just got a little bit of money. Is there anything you need?

NUT. From what?

FRANCE. From Agent Orange. They just finally paid for it, retroactive. Do you need a computer?

NUT. How about a plane ticket?

FRANCE. You can have a computer.

NUT. I'd fly to Vietnam. I'd be Johnny. Johnny Plantation Seed. I'd plant Australian plantation trees all over the countryside. All over where there used to be teak and seven shades of green. And when the foreign trees had grown so tall that the land was shaded. I'd plant the native trees all under the canopy.

Before I left I'd bring an offering of dismantled land mines to the big orange man. The orange Buddha. The Agent Orange Buddha.

He'd put his hands over his heart.

> *Shift: Vietnam. Julius is fishing with his hands. Nut is baiting a fishing pole.*

JULIUS. What?

NUT. What?

JULIUS. What're you looking at?

NUT. You.

JULIUS. Quit it.

NUT. Don't know why you're looking for fish here.

JULIUS. 'Cause I want to.
Suit yourself.

> *Silence.*

NUT. You ever think 'bout how not one of us is as we are when we're home?

JULIUS. No.

NUT. I do. I think about it all the time.
Take me for...no, take you for example. Now I have no idea what you do when you're home. Yeah, you tell me over and over what you're gonna do when you get back home. But what do you do, like usual times.

JULIUS. Well, I don't know

    Pause.

What? I don't know...same shit you do I guess.

NUT. You do NOT do the same shit I do. I doubt that you do what I do.

JULIUS. What do you do that's so special?

NUT. You. Man, I talk about myself enough. You.

    Pause.

Tell me. Come on.

JULIUS. Ah shit.
I don't know...well...okay. I build, I make model airplanes.

NUT. Model airplanes?

JULIUS. Yeah.

NUT. Like the snap-together plastic ones?

JULIUS. Nah. I build them outta balsa wood and fly them.

NUT. Oh shit.

JULIUS. I design what they're gonna look like. Sometimes put a pilot in 'em. Pick what colors, maybe stripes. Then I take them out and fly them.
I drive out to this field way out. The propeller's wound kind of like a rubber band. You have to move your finger out of the way real quick though or it gets sliced. So you wind it up wind it up tight, start the engine, hold it! Then let it go, go, go, go!
It starts racing down the field and then I chase after it with the controller in my hand.

    Nut, caught up, chases after it with Julius.

33

NUT.   JULIUS.
Go, go go!   Go, go go!

JULIUS. Then I pull the lever, the plane tips upward. It tips and up, up up! Ohhh! It's up in the air and my chest lifts up with it. Then it's up in the air.

I get scared. This is where I get scared. 'Cause they fall, you know. Sometimes they fall out of the sky and break apart. You just gotta steer it gently. Don't make any sudden moves.

> *He hands the controller to Nut.*

NUT. Don't make any sudden moves?

JULIUS. Yeah.

NUT. Got it.

> *Pause.*

So far so good!

JULIUS. So that's about it. Sometimes I also like to go fishing by myself. Mostly I like to make small things of things that used to be big things.

You? Oh, wait! I also like to dance.

NUT. I never would've thought that.

JULIUS. Yeah. Yeah, I do.

NUT. That's not who we are though. Not here.

JULIUS. No.

NUT. Maybe not there either.

JULIUS. You don't think so?

NUT. I don't get to be this kind a man there.

JULIUS. Maybe.

NUT. I see a fish.

JULIUS. Where?

NUT. Right there!

> *Julius tries to fish with his hands but fails. Nut finishes the pole and hands it to him. Bleed: Memory.*

How come we don't go fishing in Johnson's Pond?

JULIUS. Can't catch anything in there.

NUT. We don't catch anything here.

JULIUS. Fishing isn't about catching something.

NUT. Oh.

JULIUS. It's about fishing.

> *Long silence. Julius fishes in the grass.*

CRIMP. Help me. Dad's in the backyard fishing.

NUT. What?

CRIMP. Come on Dad.

NUT. Why don't you come inside?

> *Julius casts and reels.*

CRIMP. It's getting late.

NUT. Come on Dad, let's go inside.

CRIMP. You can go fishing later.

NUT. Wanna come inside with us?

CRIMP. Let's go inside now.

NUT. I'll make you coffee.

> *Julius casts and reels.*

You like coffee.

CRIMP. Come on Dad. Come on.

NUT. Let's go inside.

> *Julius casts and reels.*

Doesn't look good.

CRIMP. Dad!

JULIUS. I'm fishing.

CRIMP. Yeah, I see that.

JULIUS. I'm fishing.

CRIMP. Let's just wait for him. Wait till he's done.

> *Julius casts and reels.*

NUT. So how's work?

CRIMP. It's fine.
I got shit on.

NUT. What?

CRIMP. Yeah this one patient. I was picking him up to put him on his other side, you know so he wouldn't get bedsores?

NUT. Yeah, and he shit on you?

CRIMP. Yeah, he had the runs. I was like, I don't get paid enough for this shit.

NUT. Yeah.

CRIMP. Yeah, that's what my job's like.

> *Julius casts and reels.*

I saw a ghost once.

NUT. Yeah?

CRIMP. Yeah, no shit. I was doing my rounds and in this one room. It used to be the library. I swear to god I saw this figure. I jumped so fuckin high. I was like "Mary! Did you see that?" She was like "Come on let's go you. You and your fuckin ghosts." I don't go in there anymore.

NUT. Yeah.

So…wanna go to the gay bar with me?

CRIMP. A bar?

NUT. Yeah. Come on.

CRIMP. My husband doesn't like me to go to bars…
but I guess if it was a gay bar.

> *Julius casts and reels.*

NUT. They're having a drag king show.

CRIMP. What's that?

NUT. The opposite of a drag queen.

CRIMP. Oh.

> *Julius drops his fishing pole.*

You ready to go in now?

> *Julius shakes his head "yes."*

Come on. I'll make you coffee.

NUT. It's 2004. The same year I got a computer.

And I think…somewhere in Vietnam is a woman with her eyes popped out. She was born on the exact same day as me. She asks for a coming together. The Vietnamese people seek resolution with the American companies who manufactured Agent Orange. Among them Dow and Monsanto. The court denies their claim. Again they deny them in 2007 and 2009. The Supreme Court refuses to hear their case. Somewhere in Vietnam is a woman whose father was a soldier long dead by now.

It's death that brings my family together. When my mother's father died, my entire family went to see his body in the nursing home. When my dad got really bad, my sister came from out of state to help out, be with him. The only one who didn't come was my brother. We hadn't seen him in over ten years. He never visited, but at least he called.

JULIUS. I always regretted that I didn't visit my father in the hospital before he died.

NUT. I don't remember him.

JULIUS. No, he died when you were a baby.

NUT. I saw a picture of the both of you in your uniforms.

JULIUS. Yeah. He was in the Army. World War II

    Silence.

NUT. How did he die?

JULIUS. Intestinal cancer.

NUT. How come you didn't visit him?

JULIUS. I don't know.

    Silence.

NUT. A woman in a meeting once told me about losing her boyfriend, who she'd found later in life. She said he was amazing. Her example was that once she'd had a bad day and he drove her to the comic book store and found the comic books with Huey, Dewey, and Louie in the Junior Woodchucks. A Boy Scouts of America type thing. He told her all the answers to life were found in the *Junior Woodchucks' Guidebook*. He was right. He died in their bed. She told me that she'd kept him for a little while and that the beginning of death smelt like spices, a really pleasing sweet smell.

She was right.

When the family came to see my grandfather's body in the nursing home, his face was contorted up and to the side. His mouth was frozen open. Saliva still stretched from the top gums to the bottom gums. The room smelt like spices.

It's nice.

JULIUS. Yeah.

Silence.

NUT. It's nice that everyone is here.

JULIUS. Yeah.

NUT. I don't know who I talked to. Maybe someone in a meeting. I knew I wanted to do something special for my dad. I'd never ever given him a Father's Day card before. So I went looking for one. I got one but I never gave it to him and Father's Day passed. Then I found it and decided to give it to him anyway. It was too late.

Julius stares blankly at the card.

He read it but I don't know what he understood or didn't.
I wrote:

Happy Father's Day Dad. I want to tell you that I love you and that all the time you have been sick you have always handled it with humility and dignity. You are a power of example to me. Love Nut.

Julius puts the card down.

Three teen volunteers from hospice came to do an end-of-life video thing. By the time they came…

What's your name?

JULIUS. Julius.

NUT. How old are you?

JULIUS. I don't know.

NUT. Are you married?

JULIUS. Yes.

NUT. How did you meet your wife?

JULIUS. Ahh.

Silence.

I think...
Work.

NUT. You met at work?

JULIUS. Yeah, I think. At work I think.

NUT. Do you have any children?

JULIUS. Yes. Two. Two girls.

NUT. Is that it?

JULIUS. Yeah. They're outside.

NUT. Are you sure that's it?

JULIUS. Ah, yeah.

FRANCE. We can never show your brother this video. Your father forgot all about him.

NUT. What was one of the happiest times in your life?

     Silence.

JULIUS. Huh?

NUT. What was one of the most happiest times in your life?

JULIUS. Amm.
Ahh, what?

NUT. Do you remember a good memory?

JULIUS. Sure.

NUT. What was it?

JULIUS. I don't know. I don't remember.
It was on TV.

NUT. The TV is always on. It fills the silences. It's how we sit together.

     Nut is watching TV. Crimp calls out to them.

CRIMP. Nut!

FRANCE. Oh god.
Oh god.

NUT. Is it Grandma Lubee?

CRIMP. It must've just happened. I just just walked in.

NUT. Did it just happen?

FRANCE. Yeah.

CRIMP. I just walked in and.

FRANCE. I'm going to call the people. Call 911 and the funeral home. Before they come we should put new pajamas on her. They're soiled.

NUT. How are we going to do this.

FRANCE. Well. Let's not lift…well, we'll just cut the back off and lay this new one on her. Just help me cut them and then I'll put them on.

They do.

CRIMP. I'll getta wet rag so you can wash her.

FRANCE. Thank you.

Silence. It's awkward, and we hear the TV.

NUT. What I remember most about the day of my grandmother's death is that we didn't say a word about it. The moment the paramedics wheeled her body from the bedroom, past the living room and into the ambulance. HGTV was on.

FRANCE. I hate this decorating show.

NUT. Why?

FRANCE. Oh I just think everything they do is so gaudy.

CRIMP. I don't know. I like some of their designs.

FRANCE. Oh! It's awful.
Just you wait. Wait and see what they do with it.
They will turn it so ugly.

Shift: Vietnam.

OL BOY. What the fuck are you doing back here?

JULIUS. Chopper was full.

NUT. That don't make sense 'cause I just saw it and nobody was on it.

JULIUS. Chopper was full.

Silence.

OL BOY. Fuck man.

NUT. Well what happened. I mean in the time it took us to walk over here. What, the whole fucking chopper filled up?

JULIUS. Chopper was full.

OL BOY. Well we can't head back until you are off on a chopper on your way to where you belong. That's what the fucking deal is here.

NUT. You know what that means.

OL BOY. Stuck like a bear in honey.

NUT. No man. Time to have a little fun.

OL BOY. Aghh god.

JULIUS. When I get home I'm gonna lay around and watch TV. I'm just gonna relax, you know?

OL BOY. You might get that yet. There's another chopper comin in.

They all watch it.

NUT. Well go on.

They slap him on the back and wave goodbye. Julius walks over to it. They all watch it land. He stands there and then they watch it take off.

OL BOY. What, what was it?

JULIUS. Chopper was full.

NUT. What?

Silence.

I don't understand that. I don't understand why a full chopper would land for no fucking reason just to take off again.
You understand that?

OL BOY. No man I don't. I don't fucking understand that.

Silence.

JULIUS. Who's gonna watch your back when I'm gone?

OL BOY. We can take care of our own fucking selves.

NUT. You don't think we're tough enough to take care of ourselves?

JULIUS. At least now you don't have to miss me.

OL BOY. Rather that than you stayin in this fuckin mess.

JULIUS. You guys wanna go somewhere else?

NUT. No.   OL BOY. No.

OL BOY. No. We're gonna sit right here. We're gonna wait for another chopper.

NUT. And you're gonna get your fuck ass on it.

OL BOY. That's what we're gonna do.

Bleed: Memory. France, Crimp, and Nut all help Julius to lie down. France wipes his legs.

NUT. What's that?

FRANCE. Oh, his legs are so full of fluid that it leaks out of the pores.

NUT. Oh.

FRANCE. Okay, I'm gonna put new pajamas on him.

CRIMP. Do you need help?

FRANCE. No. No. It's your father. I can do it.

CRIMP. Ma?

FRANCE. What?

CRIMP. Are you sure?

FRANCE. Yeah.

NUT. It's okay, we can help.

FRANCE. No. No. I can do it.

CRIMP. Okay.

France cuts off his old pajamas and puts new ones on.

JULIUS. I don't want to die.

FRANCE. I know.

JULIUS. I don't want to die.

FRANCE. I know.

JULIUS. I don't want to die.

FRANCE. There's nothing I can do. I can't...I can't.

There's banging sounds.

CRIMP. Ma, you alright?

FRANCE. I'm fine

More banging. Doors. Cabinets.

NUT. What is it?

FRANCE. I can't find my keys.

More banging.

Ughhh!

NUT. I haven't seen them.

More banging.

CRIMP. Can I do anything?

FRANCE. No.

More banging.

NUT. Where are you going?

More banging.

Do you want me to go?

FRANCE. No.

NUT. Where are you going?

FRANCE. Out! I'm going out.

NUT. Is everything okay?

More banging. Louder.

FRANCE. Ughhh. Ugh.

NUT. Mom?

More banging.

Mom?

FRANCE. Nut!

NUT. Well what is it? Why are you so pissed off?

FRANCE. Jesus fucking Christ

She found her keys.

Just…just. Leave me alone.

NUT. Just tell me. Just say it.

FRANCE. Leave me alone!

France exits. Crimp shrugs her shoulders.

NUT. Why does she do that?

CRIMP. Beats me.

NUT. When someone's dying things get… Usually they don't want to die and we don't want them to die and everyone hangs on till their fingernails rip off and they plummet down the ravine. But to be selfless? To really be selfless.

Shift: Vietnam.

You gotta loosen the grip. Look what I got!

OL BOY. What?

NUT. A radio!

> *Nut presses play. A dance song from the late 1960s plays. Nut dances.*

Whooo! Come on.

OL BOY. Get outta here.

NUT. Oh no! Oh no. Listen, if we're not goin out we're gonna get fucked up right here.

> *Nut pulls out a liquor bottle.*

OL BOY. That's what I'm talkin about.

NUT. And you. You're gonna fuckin dance with me. No. No. Dance. You too. Come on come on. Fucking come on. That's it that's it.

OL BOY. Give me that.

NUT. It's your last night here. We're gonna fuck shit up. Fuck it up! Hey, hey hey. You said you liked to dance.

> *Nut dances, it becomes a mock strip dance, adolescent-boy style. They continue to dance like that and Crimp joins them. The music mixes to a contemporary dance song. Crimp grabs the bottle and drinks.*

CRIMP. Whooo!

> *Julius fades out. Bleed: Memory. Crimp and Ol Boy get a little raunchy with each other.*

This is wild!

NUT. Yeah.

CRIMP. Whooo! Whoooooo! Yeaaahhh! Take it off!

> *The club music fades out.*

NUT. This is the best drag king.

CRIMP. Yeah?

NUT. Yeah.

> *Ol Boy becomes the drag king. The music turns to a country song like Tim McGraw's "Live Like You Were Dying."**

---

* See special note on songs/recordings on page 55.

CRIMP. Oh. My. God!

NUT. Good, huh?

CRIMP. Oh my god.

NUT. What?

CRIMP. Don't you remember?

NUT. What?

CRIMP. Oh my god. Whooooo! Whooooo! Yeaahhh!

NUT. What?

CRIMP. This is the song!

NUT. What song?

CRIMP. Take it off! Whoo!

NUT. What song?

CRIMP. This is my song for Dad!

NUT. What?

CRIMP. I told you, it always makes me think of him.

NUT. Oh yeah.

CRIMP. Oh my god! Whooooo!
Wow. This drag king is…

NUT. Yeah.

CRIMP. I have to give him some money.

NUT. Do it!

CRIMP. Should I?

NUT. Why not?

CRIMP. I should…for Dad.

NUT. Yeah.

CRIMP. I'm going to! Whooooo!

> She puts money in Ol Boy's pants. Then hugs Nut for a long
> time.

What are the chances they would play that song?

NUT. Weird.

CRIMP. Yeah!

> Nut, France, and Julius stand together. Julius is looking out

blankly.

NUT. Soft-tissue sarcoma, Hodgkin's disease, prostate cancer, respiratory cancers such as lung cancer and tracheal cancer. High levels of dioxin exposure are associated with birth defects or neural tube defects, deficits in motor function, and diabetes. Paternal Agent Orange exposure can cause acute myeloid leukemia in children.

And a general decreased ability to fight off cancers.

FRANCE. I don't understand it. The doctor said this is exactly what should've worked.

NUT. I don't know.

France stares at Julius.

We should sue the VA hospital.

Silence.

We should.

FRANCE. I don't know.

NUT. It's ridiculous. Giving him laxatives for constipation when he had intestinal cancer, a gigantic tumor.

FRANCE. I know. Poor guy.

NUT. They should be shut down.

FRANCE. Well, I don't want to get into that.

NUT. Well, it's right.

FRANCE. Nut.

NUT. We should!

FRANCE. It's just not worth it.

NUT. What is?

FRANCE. For god's sake!

NUT. We should take them to court.

FRANCE. Oh god.

NUT. If they would've caught it in time.

FRANCE. Just stop.

Silence. France resumes trying to feed Julius applesauce. He won't eat it.

Come on, please.

> *He won't.*

Julius.

Please.

> *He won't.*

You have to eat something.

> *He won't.*

Just a little bit?

> *He won't and it spills on him. She wipes it up.*

Fuck!

I need your help. I just need your help.

NUT. Yeah. I'm right here. I will.

FRANCE. I just need your help.

NUT. Want me to try and feed him?

FRANCE. No.

I just need help.

NUT. What can I do?

FRANCE. I don't know. I just need help.

NUT. Well okay Mom. Okay.

FRANCE. Oh god.

> *Silence.*

I need you to watch your father.

NUT. Okay.

Come on Dad let's sit down.

> *Nut brings him to sit.*

Just stay there, please. God please.

I told a friend how I'd heard my dad say "Why doesn't anyone ever hug me anymore?" She asked me if I hugged him. I said no. On her way home from work, this friend, this seventy-five-year-old woman, stopped at my house and came inside. She'd never come into my house before. My mother father her and I stood in the doorway.

47

Awkwardly. Then suddenly after hellos and how are yous she looked at my dad and asked "Can I hug you?" He smiled. "Sure," he said.

Shift: Vietnam.

This is bullshit!

OL BOY. Motherfucker that's the third fucking chopper. You tryna tell me they've all been full? Fuck that. Fuck that shit.

NUT. I ain't signing on to that bullshit.

OL BOY. Hell naw.

JULIUS. Chopper was full.

OL BOY. Next time I don't fuckin care if it's full you're gonna get the fuck on it.

JULIUS. Peanut butter and jelly.

OL BOY. What?

JULIUS. That's what I want when I get home.

NUT. You know what the first thing I saw in Vietnam was? My first day?
Someone'd caught a Viet Cong and I went out with them to get him. He interrogated the guy but he wouldn't talk. So he stuck his knife right through his gut, but the guy still wouldn't talk.
So he took his knife like this.

Demonstrates pulling the knife up.

Slit him up. Then left him there to bleed.

OL BOY. Why the fuck are you talking about this?

NUT. 'Cause that's what I'm gonna do to him if he don't get on THAT FUCKING CHOPPER! And get outta here.

OL BOY. Shut the fuck up.

NUT. I'm telling you. I never seen anything like it in my life. Took the knife like this.

OL BOY. Shut up, man.

NUT. The shock man.

OL BOY. Shut up.

JULIUS. An Orange Julius. That's what I want.

NUT. Shocked me up right. I mean I needed that 'cause shit's crazier than that.

Took the knife like that.

JULIUS. An Orange Julius.

OL BOY. Chopper's comin in!

NUT. Right like that.

OL BOY. Chopper's comin!

JULIUS. An Orange Julius.

NUT. Right like that.

OL BOY. Chopper's comin in!

JULIUS. An Orange Julius.

NUT. Right like that.

OL BOY. Chopper's comin in!

NUT. Here's how it's gonna go down. We're gonna push that mother-fucker onto the chopper. Right like that.

OL BOY. Right like that.

Chopper's comin in!

> *Nut and Ol Boy try to get Julius in the chopper. Before he gets on, he grabs Nut.*

JULIUS. I always thought you were the better man. A good man.

> *Nut puts him on the chopper.*

NUT. Right like that.

> *They wave to him. He stands at the chopper, not moving. They push him in and Ol Boy fades out. Julius stands up.*

OL BOY. Stay there!   NUT. Stay there!

> *Bleed: Memory.*

NUT. Stay. Sit down.

> *Julius tries to stand on wobbly legs.*

Dad. Please, just sit down. You'll fall if you try and stand.

> *Julius tries to stand.*

Please.

JULIUS. I gotta go get him!

NUT. Just sit down.

JULIUS. I HAVE TO GO GET HIM!

Silence.

NUT. Okay Dad. Let's go get him. We can go get him.

Julius looks at Nut, confused. He gives up and sits down. Lies down.

My dad liked graveyards and tombstones. When he died, we didn't give him a tombstone or a memorial or even a funeral. He was cremated and put into different urns. I keep mine in my car.

He would sometimes take rubbings of tombstones he liked. Once, by himself, he visited the Vietnam Memorial Wall and he took some rubbings. I don't know where the rubbings are and I didn't ask, I didn't ask whose names were on it.

I'm nine or ten it's the same year my parents separated. My mother and I were living in a different state for a while. I hadn't seen him in a year. He drove down. Got a camper and stayed for a couple of weeks to visit me.

FRANCE. You have to go. He's your father.

NUT. I don't want to.

FRANCE. Well you have to.

NUT. *(To audience.)* I was scared of him. I'd just seen a true-life movie about a father who stole his daughter away to Iran. And the mother couldn't do anything about it. I was convinced he was going to kidnap me.

JULIUS. So what do you want to do?

NUT. I don't know.

JULIUS. Are you hungry? Want me to make you something?

NUT. No.

JULIUS. We could play cards?

NUT. I don't know.

JULIUS. Well how's school?

NUT. Fine.

JULIUS. Your mom says you're not going.

NUT. I am.

JULIUS. She said you want to stay home a lot.

NUT. I don't like it.

JULIUS. You know you have to go to school.

NUT. Yeah.

JULIUS. Want to get ice cream?

NUT. I don't know.

JULIUS. We could go in the pool. There's a pool at the campground.

NUT. Maybe later.

JULIUS. Okay.
So what've you been doing?

NUT. Nothin.

JULIUS. How do you like where you're living?

NUT. It's fine.

JULIUS. Yeah?

NUT. Yeah.

JULIUS. I've missed you.

> *Silence.*

NUT. Can my cousin come over?

JULIUS. Here? At the campground?

NUT. Yeah. Can he?

JULIUS. Today?

NUT. Yeah.

JULIUS. I guess so. We can ask.
If you want.

NUT. Yeah, I do.

I thought if my cousin was there then he wouldn't be able to kidnap me.

When they separated my folks met each other at some park with two separate cars. My dad got out to say goodbye to me and hug me but I wouldn't let him. It was the first time I ever saw him cry. But I didn't.

I feel bad because I didn't cry.

FRANCE. It's okay. You don't have to cry.

NUT. But I should've. I just didn't feel like it.

FRANCE. You don't have to cry.

NUT. My cousin came to the campground. We played in the pool and my dad threw us around so we could splash into the water. I refused to stay with him unless my cousin was there. He never kidnapped me.

On the last day of his life I crawled into bed with him.

I wish I'd never seen Shari and Lamb Chop. I whispered to him, it's alright for you to go. I wanted to do something special for him. Something selfless. He couldn't move so I put his arm around me.

I'm hugging you.

Orange powder falls onto the bed and covers them.

End of Play

PROPERTY LIST

(Use this space to create props lists for your production)

SOUND EFFECTS

(Use this space to create sound effects lists for your production)

Note on Songs/Recordings, Images, or Other Production Design Elements

Be advised that Dramatists Play Service, Inc., neither holds the rights to nor grants permission to use any songs, recordings, images, or other design elements mentioned in the play. It is the responsibility of the producing theater/organization to obtain permission of the copyright owner(s) for any such use. Additional royalty fees may apply for the right to use copyrighted materials.

For any songs/recordings, images, or other design elements mentioned in the play, works in the public domain may be substituted. It is the producing theater/organization's responsibility to ensure the substituted work is indeed in the public domain. Dramatists Play Service, Inc., cannot advise as to whether or not a song/arrangement/recording, image, or other design element is in the public domain.

NOTES
(Use this space to make notes for your production)